TIPS FROM YOUR JOB COACH

...A STRATEGIC GUIDE FOR EMPLOYMENT SEEKERS

Dona M. Woodley

DIAMOND MEDIA PRESS CO.
1-888-322-7392
https://www.diamondmediapressco.com/

Copyright © 2020

By Dona M. WOODLEY

All rights reserved.

ISBN Paperback: 978-1-951302-31-3

DEDICATION

This work is dedicated to all of the single Mothers and Fathers who are in search of employment; to all of the service women and men who have returned home and are now looking for employment, to all of the high school and college students and technical school students who are going out into the world of work, to women and men returning to the workforce to support their families, This work is dedicated to the workers who were employment but due to COVID-19 find themselves unable to return to their jobs. This work is dedicated to the women and men who are not entrepreneurs and find great satisfaction in trading a hard day's work for an honest paycheck.

Always know that change is always changing. Be ready for change because it is the only constant in the world. Be adaptable, stay trainable, and prepare yourself for advancement.

Table of Contents

Dona will always give important facts, not fiction in reference to employment. I am a former Retail Store Manager and she has vast internal knowledge of how corporate hiring is handled today. Read, Listen & Learn, you will be the benefactor 100%.

~Raymond Darryl Cox

PREFACE

Getting Past the Gatekeeper

Do you think like a salesperson when looking for employment? When searching for employment it may be wise to do what sales people do. You're the product you are selling.

Get to know your prospective employer A good sales person must know their potential client. You must know your potential employer.

Although it may be impossible to tailor your pitch to employers, you can do some research to find out what skills they are in the market for. Hiring managers get frustrated when sitting in an interview with a job-seeker who has little knowledge or understanding of the company. Do your research! There's just no excuse not to have a good understanding about the company for whom you are seeking employment. You can get so much information from the company website: find out what their mission is, where they're going, and as much as you can about their product or service or see if anyone in your network knows someone who works there, and who can give you some insight. Once you've done your research, not only can you can tailor your skills and experience appropriately, you'll also look more knowledgeable in an interview.

Ask questions and Listen to the answers.

Did you know that a salesperson speaks 20% of the time. They ask questions and listens to the answers during 80% of the time.

A good sales person knows that when you ask questions you control the conversation. A good employment interview allows plenty of time to communicate your value. When the interviewer asks you if you have any questions you should have prepared at least 5 questions. These questions should be a combination about the company in general and specific questions about the position for which you are applying. So in preparation for your employment interview you need to jot down some questions in advance and then add to it as questions arise throughout the interview

Make yourself stand out by differentiation top salespeople know their competition. They find out all they can about their competitors' offering – the features, the benefits, the drawbacks…everything. Why? So they can best differentiate themselves. They know buyers have any number of options, so the only way to capture that market share is to offer something the competition doesn't.

When it comes to job hunting – you're the product. Find out what makes you unique, and make that a key focus of your "pitch". Maybe the company is expanding internationally, and you worked or studied abroad. Or maybe you have an industry blog – and an established following – that could be used to the company's advantage. Sell it!

Not only will they see your unique offering as a benefit, they'll remember you. And guess what happens to memorable people… they get called in for a first, second or third interview.

The salesperson builds a rapport with the gatekeeper or finds ways to bypass them entirely. It's their job to do whatever they can to stop a salesperson from getting through. Salespeople have lots of tricks to get in the door and nothing can stop them.

The Gate Keeper is anyone standing between you and the prospective employer-the boss-the person who is conducting the interview. In sales it's the decision maker. For you it's the receptionist or executive assistant the HR manager or even a nondescript email alias.

The gatekeeper's job is to screen correspondence-hence your resume. So, how do you make sure your resume is seen by the person hiring? You could call the company directly and ask the name of the person hiring for the position sought. You may not get an answer, but at least you gave it a shot. Another is to research the department itself and find out. Try and find out what their email address might be. This may not be as difficult as you would think. Once you figure that out email your resume directly to them

Follow-Up.

A sale is an ongoing process. It involves a series of steps over a period of time. In a tough economy customers who would usually make a purchase will now stop and think carefully if it's the exact thing they need. The recession delays employers in making impulsive hires. They have plenty of resumes from candidates to choose from than in a good economy. No matter the state of the economy, the person hiring is probably very busy dealing with some of their more mission focused daily responsibilities. For this reason alone it is critical that you follow-up because they may just forget you.

If you haven't heard from them within a week of sending your resume, or your interview, send a follow-up email, briefly reiterating your qualifications (or something you forgot to mention in the interview). Doing so will communicate just how interested you are in the job, and will keep you fresh in their memory. But following up isn't easy. You'll have to keep track of your correspondence – particularly the more promising ones – in order to remember who to follow up with, and when.

It sounds like a lot of work, but it's certainly not a waste of time. Just like in sales, following up with an existing lead is more cost (and time) effective than chasing down a brand new one. Turning a No into a Yes The salesperson's mantra is that each rejection brings you a step closer to success. They expect a certain number of rejections before they will see success. Job hunting is the same. You will face rejections repeatedly before getting hired. Keep it up though. All it takes is one "yes" for a successful search for employment.

Good luck in your search for employment.

What Are You Made Of?

When looking for employment, you are the product you are selling. Just like advertisers need to know how to package goods that consumers will be attracted to, you must package yourself in a way that will attract employers to you. Proper and effective packaging is key. How can you make your product (YOU) stand out?

Packaging

The packaging on the candy bar is a good start. It's eye-catching colors and descriptive words draw attention. All the things candy lovers are looking for. But what are employers looking for? Choose your words carefully and accurately. Using words that will interest the companies you apply to will grab their attention. That's why you need an effective résumé.

What you have to offer---the ingredients

Just like a recipe to a candy bar your résumé contains unique ingredients. YOU'RE SKILLS.
What makes you unique to the position?
Skills can be grouped into three categories:
Skills learned through past experience and education (knowledge-based skills): computer skills, marketing skills, communication skills, management skills, product development, etc.
Skills you bring with you to any job (transferable or portable skills): customer focus, organizational skills, writing skills, coordination, team leader, problem solving, budgets and numbers, time management, etc.
Personal traits, the things that make you who you are: quick learner, self-motivated, friendly, organized good attitude, good judgement, flexible, creative, independent, etc.

Divide a sheet of paper into three columns and lable them according to the three types of skills listed above. List your skills in the appropriate column. Now you have something to work with when putting together an effective résumé. You still have some work to do before you can take your product to market, but at least you are off to a great start!

TIP #1 SIX STEPS TO YOUR SEARCH FOR EMPLOYMENT

Assess your skills and interest.

Do you have relevant work experience?
Have you completed recent training?
Do you have effective communication skills?
Do you possess proficient computer skills?
Do you have extensive product knowledge?

Match your skills and interest with career possibilities.
Some employers hire individuals because they have entry level skills. Entry level positions are a foot in the door.

Learn about the company before submitting an employment application. Ask about a company's Mission Statement; then, decide if you agree with its philosophy.

What part of your work do you value? Do you prefer to work alone or as part of a team? Some individuals prefer to compete with others. Others enjoy making decisions.

Decide on which fields you want to pursue.
You may be multitalented and capable of pursuing more than one career; but it is best to decide on which direction you would like to concentrate your career.

Formulate a strategic plan.
 Planning your job search is an important step. Set goals. Plan ways to accomplish your   goals, then do it.

Set your time table.
If your goal is to become employed within six weeks, conduct an aggressive job search that   will yield at least three or four interviews per week. Plan each step, and monitor your progress.

Follow up on everything.
Follow up on networking efforts, telephone interviews, word of mouth leads, information interviews, résumé mailings and other employment opportunities.

Exercise 1

I.   **<u>Assess your skills and interest.</u>**

1.   What kind of work experience do you possess?

2.   Have you completed any sort of career training? Explain.

3.   What computer skills, if any, do you possess?

4.   What other equipment or machines can you operate proficiently?

5.   Do you enjoy communicating with others?

6.   What type of work are you interested in?

7.   Why are you interested in this type of work?

II.   **<u>Match your skills and interest with career possibilities.</u>**

1.   What part of your work do you value most? Why?

2.   What part of your work do you value least? Why?

III.   **<u>Decide on which field you want to pursue.</u>**

Do you possess more than one skill? If so, which skill do you plan to pursue as a career choice?

TIP #2 DEVELOP YOUR STRATEGIC PLAN

Your first step is to set your short-term goal (getting a job) and your long-term goal (where you want your career to go). Develop your strategic plan. It will serve as your map to where you want to go in the short and long terms. Focus on your long-term success. There are a wide variety of job search strategies and resources available to get you from here to there. Use them.

The Internet

Modern technology has introduced a whole new way to approach your employment search. You can 'surf the net' to find advertised job listings. You can also post your résumé on the internet. Monster.com, Careerlinks.com, Jobnet.com are three of the commonly used online résumé posting links. They each offer job search tips.

Human Resource Departments

Call several prospective employers, and request an information interview. Ask for permission to view their bulletin board for vacant positions.

Community Bulletin Boards

People often place ads on community bulletin boards. These can be found in places like the public library, post offices, and supermarkets. Post your own ad on a bulletin board.

Career Fairs

The local newspaper, radio stations, and the internet usually advertise Career fairs. Attend as many as you can, and always carry at least 20 résumés with you. Be prepared to talk about yourself.

Volunteer work

Offer volunteer services for a specified period of time. You can learn from the experience, and you'll have the opportunity to impress the employer; and you may be offered employment.

Information Interviews

The purpose of an information interview is to meet with a contact person. Information interviewing or 'networking' is a viable way to conduct a career market research, to refine career goals, and to uncover vacancy information in an industry or a geographical region. Information interviewing requires solid preparation, sincerity, and much effort. The networking letter is the first step in the information interviewing process. A résumé is not attached to a networking letter; however, you may present your résumé at the interview to help the interviewer address your questions.

Word of mouth

Many of your friends have jobs. Ask if their company is hiring. Ask if they know of any employers who are hiring.

The Yellow Page Telephone Directory

The Yellow Pages telephone directory gives information about businesses in your community. It is another source to check when looking for a career. The Yellow Pages can help you select employers based on your areas of interest. To use the Yellow Pages, look up a topic of interest, then look below that heading to find companies you would like to contact.

Career Centers

Career Centers are supported by the government. They receive no fee. Career Centers help people find jobs in and out of the government.
Every city or town in the United States has at least one Career Center. You have the opportunity to search their computers for available positions.

You also have the opportunity to post your résumé onto their network. When you choose these options, prospective employers have the chance to download your résumé and contact you directly.

Employment Agencies

Employment agencies fall into three categories: private, public, and temporary.

Public employment agencies are supported by the government. They are now called Career Centers.

Private employment agencies are also businesses that assist job seekers find employment. They usually charge a fee. Private employment agencies run advertisement in the classified section of the newspaper. Sometimes, these ads list the amount of the fee job seekers are expected to pay the employment agency for the advertised position. Other times, the ad list the fee as "fee paid." The fee is either paid by the potential employer after hiring an applicant or the fee is paid the applicant upon agreement after signing a contract with the agency. Ask the representative how and when the fee is paid.

Temporary employment agencies employ individuals to work for organizations on a temporary basis. The assignment could run anywhere from one day to long term. A temporary position can turn into a full-time position. It is an opportunity to demonstrate your skills and abilities, and to network. Temporary employment agencies offer job training in a variety of fields. Check with your local temporary employment office to learn what services are offered.

Classified Newspaper Advertisements

The classified section of the newspaper 'help wanted ads' is the most common way to look for employment. There are two types of help wanted ads. The closed ad lists the position, the person to mail a response to, and the post office box to respond to.

The closed ad rarely states the name of the company, description of expected responsibilities, salary, or work hours. The other type of help wanted ad is the open ad. The open ad lists the name of the company, salary, hours (sometimes), some of the expected responsibilities, some of the benefits, the person to respond to, and a telephone number.

The job search is one of the most important steps in your work career. Knowing how and where to find a job is a valuable skill. As a new worker, you should be careful in your choice of employment. The job you choose may last for many years. Think carefully before making a career choice. Study the companies in your area. Ask questions about the kinds of jobs they offer. When looking for a job, use as many sources of information as you can.

Exercise 2

TIP #2 DEVELOP YOUR STRATEGIC PLAN

Discuss and then answer the following questions.

1.	How can you use the Internet to assist you in your employment search?

2.	Who would you contact to view postings of vacant employment positions?

3.	How are Community Bulletin Boards used in a search for employment?

4.	What may happen if you offer to volunteer at a company for a specified period of time?

5.	What is the purpose of an information interview?

6.	What is required for successful information interviewing?

7.	Should you attach your résumé with a networking letter?

8.	What is the purpose of telling your employed friends that you are looking for employment?

9.	Job Centers are supported by the_____________________.

10.	What can happen when you post your résumé on the computer at a Job Center?

11.	How is the Yellow Page directory used to conduct a job search?

12.	Name at least three types of employment agencies.

13.	Which type of employment agency charges a fee for finding a job for job seekers?

14.   What are the advantages of working for temporary employment agencies?

15.   Discuss the differences between an 'open ad' and a 'closed ad' for employment listed in the Classified section of the local newspaper.

TIP #3 WHAT EMPLOYERS WANT

Increasingly, in today's workplace, employees work together to successfully complete projects. As a Job Coach, I have had the opportunity to ask many employers what they wanted from an employee. Nine out of ten responded the same:

Oral communication skills — The ability to effectively express oneself verbally.

Interpersonal skills — The ability to get along with others.

Analytical skills — The ability to think and problem solve.

Team work — The ability to work as part of a team.

Flexibility — The willingness to accept change.

Written communication skills — The ability to communicate through writing.

Leadership qualities — The ability to take control, if and when necessary.

Trainability — The ability to learn new skills.

Exercise 3

TIP #3 WHAT EMPLOYERS WANT

Discuss and explain the importance of each item listed:

1. Oral communication skills – the ability to effectively express oneself verbally.

2. Interpersonal skills – the ability to get along with others.

3. Analytical skills – the ability to think and problem solve.

4   Team work – the ability to work as part of a team.

5   Flexibility – the willingness to accept change.

6   Written communication skills - the ability to communicate through writing.

7   Leadership qualities – the ability to take control, if and when necessary.

8   Trainability – the ability to learn new skills

TIP #4 UNCOVER YOUR ABILITIES

Most people have more to offer an employer than they realize. The problem is, many people find it difficult to identify those 'soft skills.' Here are some suggestions on how you can uncover your hidden abilities, and bring them to the attention of an employer.

<u>Look at your high school and college extracurricular activities.</u>
Being member of the debate team, having participated in drama club, or having worked on campus newspaper or yearbook committee showcase your ability to communicate effectively – both orally and in writing. Participating in these activities demonstrate other key traits, such as flexibility. If you've played sports, you've got an activity tailor-made to demonstrate your ability to work in a team. If you hold a leadership role in an extracurricular club or activity, be sure to highlight that.

<u>Look at your course work, internships, co-op experiences.</u>
Cooperative education experiences, at any level, should be included in your description of your skills. They show work experience, team work, leadership, initiative, and a willingness to work.

<u>Community involvement</u>
Have you ever worked on a class project or used your analytical abilities in your course work? These are examples of team-work and analytical thinking abilities. Have you ever spoken to a civic, or church group? The Girls Scouts, Boy Scouts, karate classes, clubs, and even some after school programs help youth to develop public speaking skills and leadership skills. Have you ever worked on a community project such as building a house or park in your neighborhood? Have you tutored someone in reading, math, computers, or some other area?

<u>Look at your part time jobs and volunteer work.</u>
While your part time jobs or volunteer work experiences may not be directly relevant to your career goals, they may well have helped you acquire some of the skills employers are looking for. Have you ever worked in a fast food restaurant or convenience store? This experience in public relations and operating a cash register will be of some interest to some employers.

Exercise 4

TIP #4 UNCOVER YOUR ABILITIES

1.	High school and college extracurricular activities.

	Think back when you were in high school. What activities outside of your regular coursework were you involved in?

2.	Did you have a job while attending high school, college or training program? Describe.

3.	Were you an active member in your community? What type of community activities were you involved in? Be specific.

4.	What part-time job have you held, if any? Describe in detail.

5.	Have you participated in volunteer work? Describe in detail.

TIP #5 YOUR COVER LETTER

Your cover letter serves more than one purpose. It is the employer's first impression of you. It is a concrete demonstration of your written communication skills. It is an introduction to the employer. Your cover letter is an extension of your résumé. By carefully considering the purposes and impact of every letter you write, you can enhance your employability. Structure your cover letter with three or four paragraphs.

When writing your cover letter, remember to following guidelines:

1. Come to the point. Reveal your purpose and interest.
2. Make reference to your résumé.
3. Outline your strongest qualifications that match the employer's requirements.
4. Convince the employer that you have the personal qualifications and motivation to perform well in the position. Sell yourself.
5. Suggest an action plan. Request an interview.
6. Show appreciation for his/her time and consideration.
7. Remind the receiver of your résumé.

The following sample cover letters are examples of the above seven rules. The first cover letter is written in the *block style.* Begin One inch from the top of the page, type your return address. Double space and type the current date. Double space and type the company's address. Double space and type the first paragraph. Double space between each paragraph. Leave two spaces between sincerely and your name, then type your name. Skip down four spaces and type the words *enclosure: résumé.* Sign your name between sincerely and your typed name.

Exercise 5

Letter Writing

When writing any type of letter, it is necessary to use the proper format. Employers notice the format of the cover letter, the thank you letter, and the rejection letter. Use one of the following formats for writing your letters. Be consistent. If you choose to use the modified block letter format for your cover letter, then use the modified block letter format for all of your correspondence.

Block Letter

Type your return address 16 lines or 1 inch from the top of the page. The telephone number is optional at this phase. Skip 2 lines before typing the recipient's address along the left margin. There should be 2 spaces between the recipient's address, the date, the salutation, the paragraphs, the closing, and the enclosures.

Sample Cover Letter 1: Block Style

Joe Outta Work
8900 Pleasehelp Lane
Employment line. NJ 99887
Email: Joeouttawork@hotmail.com

January 14, 1999

Ms. Cynthia Norvales
Hansel & Sons Delivery
1235 Narrowneck. MA 87653

I read your company's description on your web page and would like to inquire about employment opportunities in your truck drivers training and employment program.

As you review my enclosed resume, yo will find that I have extensive knowledge of some of the delivery routes your company uses. I traveled across country twenty-two times over the past three years. I enjoy long distance driving.

While I have yet to drive a eighteen wheeler. I have driven a motorcycle, a car and a bus across country. I have a clean driving record and I am willing to learn your methos of long distance driving.

Would you please consider my request for a personal interview to discuss further my qualifications and to learn more about this opportunity?

I shall call you next week to see if a meeting can be arranged. Should you need to reach me, please feel free to call me at (000) 667- 0098. If I am not in, please leave a message on my answering machine and I will call you withing a day.

Thank you for your consideration. I look forward to talking with you.

Sincerely
Joe Outta Work
Joe Outta Work

Enclose resume

1. Come to the point. Reveal your purpose and interest.

2. Make reference to your resume.

3. Outline your strongest qualifications that match the employer's requirements.

4. Convince the employer that have the personal qualifications and motivation to perform well in the position. Sell yourself.

5. Suggest an action plan. Request an interview.

6. Show appreciation for his/ her time and consideration.

7. Remind the reciever of your resume

Modified Letter

Type your return address 16 lines or 1 inch from the top of the page. The telephone number is optional at this phase. Skip 2 lines before typing the recipient's address along the left margin. There should be 2 spaces between the recipient's address, the date, the salutation, the paragraphs, the closing and the enclosures. The date is typed in the middle of the page. Each paragraph should be indented 5 spaces.

<u>Sample Cover Letter 2: Modified Block Style</u>

Mary Jo Needajob
2232 Sisco Avenue
Freeport, VA 99900

February 27, 1999

Mrs. Cecelia McDuffie
Human Resources Manager
4345 Statton Plaza Suite #3
Freeport, VA 99000

Dear Mrs. McDuffie:

I am writing this letter in response to your February 27, 1998 advertisment in the Freeport Gazette for entry level Computer Operator.

As you review my resume you will find that I possess the necessary skills to fill your vacant position. Your position requires knowledge of Micro Soft Word 97, Lotus 1-2-3, and organizational skills. I have completed the computer course at my high school and have acquired mastery of Micro Soft Word 97, Lotus 1-2-3 and Excel. My key- boarding skills exceed 65 words per minute.

IAdditionaly, I worked as a cooperative education student in computing operation for a large bank where I gained knowledge in financial systems.

I would appreciate a personal interview to discuss your qualifications and my experience in detail. I can be reached at the above address and telephone number at your earliest convenience.

Thank you for your consideration. I look forward to bearing frim you.

Truly Yours,
Mary Jo Needjob
Mary Jo Needajob

Enclosure: resume

1. Come to the point. Reveal your purpose and interest.

2. Make reference to your resume.

3. Outline your strongest qualifications that match the employer's requirements.

4. Convince the employer that you have the personal qualifications and motivation to perform well in the position. Sell yourself.

5. Suggest an action plan. Request an interview.

6. Show appreciation for his/her time and consideration.

7. Remind the reciever of your resume

Like the block letter, the modified block letter begins one inch from the top of the page. The date is centered two spaces after your return address. Double space and type the company name and address. Double space and type the greeting followed by a comma. Double space and indent each paragraph. Because the letter is indented, it can be typed single spaced.

Hint: Always use a contact name in your cover letter unless otherwise stated.

TIP #5 YOUR COVER LETTER

In the space below, structure a cover letter using the examples on the previous two pages. Make your cover letter at least three paragraphs long. Check your spelling, grammar and punctuation.

Write your cover letter here.

Think Like A Salesperson When Looking For Employment!

When searching for employment it may be wise to do what sales people do. You are the product you are selling. Get to know your prospective employer A good sales person must know their potential client. You must know your potential employer.

Although it may be impossible to tailor your pitch to employers, you can do some research to find out what skills they are in the market for. Hiring managers get frustrated when sitting in an interview with a job-seeker who has little knowledge or understanding of the company. Do your research! There's just no excuse not to have a good understanding about the company for whom you are seeking employment. You can get so much information from the company website: find out what their mission is, where they're going, and as much as you can about their product or service or see if anyone in your network knows someone who works there, and who can give you some insight. Once you've done your research, not only can you can tailor your skills and experience appropriately, you'll also look more knowledgeable in an interview.

Ask questions and Listen to the answers.

Did you know that a salesperson speaks 20% of the time. They ask questions and listens to the answers during 80% of the time. A good sales person knows that when you ask questions you control the conversation.

A good employment interview allows plenty of time to communicate your value. When the interviewer ask you if you have any questions you should have prepared at least 5 questions.
These questions should be a combination about the company in general and specific questions about the position for which you are applying.

So in preparation for you employment interview you need to jot down some questions in advance and then add to it as questions arise throughout the interview.

Make Yourself Stand Out by Differentiation Top salespeople know their competition. They find out all they can about their competitors' offering – the features, the benefits, the drawbacks…everything. Why? So they can best differentiate themselves. They know buyers have any number of options, so the only way to capture that market share is to offer something the competition doesn't.

When it comes to job hunting – you're the product. Find out what makes you unique, and make that a key focus of your "pitch". Maybe the company is expanding internationally, and you worked or studied abroad. Or maybe you have an industry blog – and an established following – that could be used to the company's advantage. Sell it!

Not only will they see your unique offering as a benefit, they'll remember you. And guess what happens to memorable people… they get called in for a first, second or third interview.

Getting past the Gate Keeper The salesperson builds a rapport with the gatekeeper or finds ways to bypass them entirely. It's their job to do whatever they can to stop a salesperson from getting through. Salespeople have lots of tricks to get in the door and nothing can stop them.

The Gate Keeper is anyone standing between you and the prospective employer-the boss-the person who is conducting the interview. In sales it's the decision maker. For you it's the receptionist or executive assistant the HR manager or even a nondescript email alias.

The gatekeeper's job is to screen correspondence-hence your resume. So, how do you make sure your resume is seen by the person hiring? You could call the company directly and ask the name of the person hiring for the position sought. You may not get an answer, but at least you gave it a shot. Another is to research the department itself and find out. Try and find out what their email address might be. This may not be as difficult as you would think. Once you figure that out email your resume directly to them.

Follow-Up.

A sale is an ongoing process. It involves a series of steps over a period of time. In a tough economy customers who would usually make a purchase will now stop and think carefully if it's the exact thing they need. The recession delays employers in making impulsive hires. They have plenty of resumes from candidates to choose from than in a good economy. No matter the state of the economy, the person hiring is probably very busy dealing with some of their more mission focused daily responsibilities. For this reason alone it is critical that you follow-up because they may just forget you.

If you haven't heard from them within a week of sending your resume, or your interview, send a follow-up email, briefly reiterating your qualifications (or something you forgot to mention in the interview). Doing so will communicate just how interested you are in the job, and will keep you fresh in their memory. But following up isn't easy. You'll have to keep track of your correspondence – particularly the more promising ones – in order to remember who to follow up with, and when.

It sounds like a lot of work, but it's certainly not a waste of time. Just like in sales, following up with an existing lead is more cost (and time) effective than chasing down a brand new one.

Turning a No into a Yes The salesperson's mantra is that each rejection brings you a step closer to success. They expect a certain number of rejections before they will see success. Job hunting is the same. You will face rejections repeatedly before getting hired. Keep it up though. All it takes is one "yes" for a successful search for employment.

Good luck in your search for employment.

TIP #6 YOUR RÉSUMÉ

Use the space below to write a rough draft of your résumé.

Objective: What position are you applying for?

Skills: List your skills here. Remember to list skills gained through volunteer work, part-time employment, community work; equipment you know how to operate; communication skills; leadership skills; and skills gained through work experience.

1.
2.
3.
4.
5.

Education: List your high school first, then all other institutions of learning. This includes college, trade school, on the job training, workshops, seminars, in-service training, etc. Remember the complete names, locations and dates completed.

1.
2.
3.
4.
5.

Employment History: Begin with your last or current employment. List the name of the company, the location, (complete address, including zip code), the dates you worked there, telephone number, name of your supervisor, and your job title. Describe your job in detail.

1.
2.
3.
4.
5.

Awards, honors, and certificates: This section is optional.

Military: This section is optional.

References: List at least three references. Include complete names, titles, addresses, telephone numbers, fax numbers, and, if applicable, e-mail addresses. All references should be of a professional nature. List past employers, counselors, teachers, or instructors. If you have been out of the job market for an extended period of time, you may use community representatives such as politicians or clergy. Avoid listing relatives as references.

Use the space provided to list at least three employment references. Remember, use past employers and community volunteer work. You may also use high school counselors or social workers if you have been looking for work for an extended period of time.

<u>Sample reference listings</u>

Donald McDaniel, Owner Mr. Charles Holland

McDaniels Hamburgers, Counselor
223 Daven Highway Rockland
Senior High School
Freeport, VA 18776 777 Rockland Drive
(000) 887-9865
Email:McDanielsHamburgers@Burgers.com

Now use a separate sheet to compose your résumé.

TIP #7 YOUR PORTFOLIO

A portfolio is a good tool to take with you on a job interview. Organized neatly, a portfolio demonstrates organizational skills, and enhances the interview by inviting the interviewer into your personal life (to an extent). It makes the interview go smoother by enabling you to talk about yourself. Use a new lose-leaf binder to arrange your portfolio. Use plastic page pockets to preserve your documents. Include these items:

<u>Recent high school graduates should include:</u>

Résumé Diploma Transcript
Awards, certificates, accommodations
Reference letters from employers, counselors, and teachers
Writing samples (an English class project, for example)
Photographs at work (especially co-op students)
Photographs or samples of your best project

<u>Individuals who have been out of high school for over two years should include:</u>

Résumé
College/Trade school diploma or certificate of completion Transcripts
High School diploma and transcript (optional)
Reference letters
Certificates of completion, accommodations, merit awards, Employee of the Month award
Other awards from work, e.g. seminars, workshops, in-service training
Your portfolio will be of great assistance to you during the job interview. The portfolio   provides proof of your accomplishments. It is also an excellent way to organize your documents.
If you find yourself searching for words during the interview, use your portfolio as a guide. Present a neatly typed portfolio after the interview has begun, usually when the employer asks what you've accomplished in your career.

Exercise 7

<u>Prep your portfolio</u>

TIP #8 – YOU'RE EMPLOYMENT INTERVIEW

If you are prepared, the employment interview can be a good experience. In preparation for the employment interview, the following steps are suggested:

Get a good night's rest
Be well groomed

Women should:

Wear a dark suit or dress.

Wear modern, yet conservative hairstyles.

Wear minimum cosmetics.

Wear a minimum amount of conservative jewelry.

Wear a conservative amount of perfume.

Men should:

Wear a dark suit with a tie.

Wear a minimum amount of cologne.

Wear modern, yet conservative hairstyles.

Wear minimum amount of jewelry.

- ☐ Bring your neatly typed résumés, portfolio (optional), paper, pen with black ink, and calendar/appointment book.
- ☐ Eat a well-balanced breakfast.
- ☐ Research the company.
- ☐ Prepare questions to ask the interviewer.
- ☐ Arrive on time. It is a good idea to be at least 10 minutes early for the interview.

- ☐ Sit only after being invited to do so.
- ☐ Have a firm handshake.
- ☐ Introduce yourself in a courteous manner.
- ☐ Read company material while waiting.
- ☐ Remember that the receptionist may be watching you. (Pre-screening)
- ☐ Use body language to show interest.
- ☐ Look at the interviewer's nose.
- ☐ Smile, nod, and give nonverbal feedback.
- ☐ Be prepared to talk about yourself.
- ☐ Be prepared to fill out an employment application, usually prior to the beginning of the interview.
- ☐ Use a black ball point pen.
- ☐ Write a thank-you letter to anyone you have spoken to.

Questions you may be asked during an interview:

1. What do you know about this company?
2. What can you offer this company?
3. Why should I hire you?
4. Where do you see yourself in the next five years?
5. How do you keep a positive attitude during a difficult situation?
6. In your past job, have you had to make an important decision? Explain.
7. How would you handle multiple tasks? How would you organize your work?
8. What experience do you have in this field?
9. How would you describe your last boss?
10. How do you spend your spare time?
11. Are you willing to begin at the entry level?
12. Are you authorized to work in this country?
13. How do you feel about teamwork?
14. What is your understanding of customer service?
15. Are you willing to work independently?
16. Are you prepared to learn new things?
17. What formal training have you had?
18. Are you willing to work evening and weekend hours?
19. How do you feel about a highly customer responsive assignment? Give an example.
20. What has been your experience with customer service?
21. Why do you want to come to work for us?
22. Tell me about your experiences with teamwork in your last job.
23. Tell me about a few of your key decision-making experiences in your last assignment.
24. What is best about you when you are working with others?
25. How do you feel about sharing your ideas with others?
26. We are a company focused on continuous improvement. What improvements have you made at your previous company or organization?

Be prepared.

The time to ask the questions you have prepared for the interview is when the interviewer asks, "Do you have any questions for me?"

<u>Ask the Human Resource Manager:</u> (Usually the first interview)

1. Would you please explain the benefit package for this position?
2. Are employees encouraged and given the opportunity to express their ideas and concerns?
3. What do employees seem to like best and least about the company?
4. What is the rate of employee turnover?
5. How large is the department where the opening exists?
6. Does the job require much travel?
7. How are employees who travel compensated?
8. What are the chances of being relocated after starting the job?
9. What type of orientation or training do new employees receive?
10. How long is the probationary period for new employees?
11. How often are performance reviews given?
12. Who determines raises and promotions, and how is this determined?
13. What are the long-range possibilities for employees in similar positions who consistently perform above expectations?
14. What is the company's longevity?
15. How long has the company been in this community?
16. Is this company considering downsizing in the foreseeable future?

<u>Ask your prospective supervisor:</u> (Usually the second interview)

1. What would be my primary responsibilities?
2. What would I be expected to accomplish in the first six months on the job? In the first year?
3. What are some of the department's ongoing and anticipated special projects?
4. How much contact or exposure does the department and staff have with management?

<u>Ask a prospective co-worker</u> (ask in the lobby, at the elevator, in the hall)

1. What do you like best/least about working for this department /company?
2. Can you describe a typical workday in the department?
3. Do you feel free to express your ideas and concerns here?
4. What are the possibilities for professional growth and promotion?
5. How much interaction do you have with superiors, colleagues, and customers?
6. How long have you been with the company?

__Hint:__ Oftentimes, the receptionist is the interviewer's pre-screener. Think about how you present yourself to him/her. This includes the initial telephone interview through to the personal interview. Are you chewing gum, smoking, reading a newspaper or looking around? Are your clothes clean and neat? The receptionist may report his/her initial perception of you to the interviewer. If you are prepared, this could work to your advantage.

TIP #9 LEGAL AND ILLEGAL EMPLOYMENT INTERVIEW QUESTIONS

The federal, state, and local laws regulate the questions a prospective employer may ask a job candidate. An employer's questions, whether on the job application or during the testing process, must be related to the job you are applying for.

<u>The employer's focus must be:</u> What do I need to know to decide whether this person can perform the functions of this job?

If you are asked an illegal question you have three options:

1. You can answer the question. You are free to do so, if you wish. However, if you choose to answer an illegal question, you are giving information that is not related to the job. You could answer incorrectly, and therefore, harm your chances of getting the job.

2. You can refuse to answer the question, which is well within your rights. Unfortunately, you run the risk of coming across as uncooperative or confrontational; but this also depends on how you word your refusal.

3. You can examine the question for its intent and respond with an answer as it might apply to the job.

Examples:
"Are you a US citizen?"
"I am authorized to work in this country."
"Who will care for your children while you are working?"
"I can meet the work schedule that this job requires."

The following chart shows examples of some illegal and legal questions.

Inquiry	Illegal Questions	Legal Questions
Age	How old are you? What is your birthdate? When were you born?	Are you over the age of 18? May I see your ID?

National Origin or Citizenship	Are you a citizen of the U.S.? Where were you or your parents born? What is your native tongue?	Are you authorized to work in the U.S.? What languages do you speak fluently? (This question is OK if this ability is relevant to the job performance).
Personal	What clubs or social organizations do you belong to?	List any professional or trade groups or other organizations that you might consider relevant to your ability to perform this job.
Age	How tall are you? How much do you weigh? (Questions about height and weight are only acceptable if minimum standards are essential to the safe performance of the job.)	Are you able to lift 50 pounds and carry it 100 yards, as part of the job?
Disabilities	Do you have any disabilities? Please complete the following medical history. Have you had any recent or past illness/operations? If yes, list them and give dates when these occurred. What was the date of your last physical? How is your family's health? When did you lose your hearing? Do you need any accommodations to perform the job? (These questions can only be asked after a job offer has been made).	Are you able to perform the essential functions of this job? (This question is OK if the interviewer has thoroughly described the job). Can you demonstrate how you would perform the following job-related function? As part of the hiring process you may be required to undergo a medical exam. (Exam results remain confidential; however, medical safety personnel may be informed if medical treatment is required, as supervisors may be informed about necessary accommodations based on exam results).
Arrest Record	Have you ever been arrested?	Have you ever been convicted of ? (The crime named should be reasonably related to the performance of the job in question).
Military	If you've been in the military, were you honorably discharged?	In what branch of the Armed Forces did you serve? What type of training did you receive?

During an employment interview, answer only the legal questions you may be asked. Answer only the legal questions below:

1. What can you offer this company?

2. Why should I hire you?

3. Where do you see yourself in five years? Ten years? (Long term goals)

4. How long have you had to use that cane?

5. How do you keep a positive attitude during a difficult situation?

6. In your past job, have you had to make an important decision? Explain.

7. Who will care for your children if you are suddenly asked to work overtime?

8. What did you like most about your last job?

9. What did you like least about your last job?

10. Did you play competitive sports in school?

11. Do you consider yourself a fast learner? Explain.

12. What was the last book you read?

13. How well do you work under pressure?

14. If I were to talk to your former co-workers, how would they describe you?

15. How long have you lived in this city?

16. Would your spouse be concerned if you were to do any business travel?

17. Have you ever been fired?

18. What did you think of your last supervisor?

19. Do you consider yourself a perfectionist?

20. Why did you leave your last position?

21. What are your career goals?

22. Why were you fired from your last job?

23. What are your short-term goals?

24. How long will it take you to learn this job?

25. How long do you intend to stay on this job?

26. What you would find most difficult about this job?

27. What was your salary in your last position?

28. Do you have references?

29. Why are you applying for this job?

30. What experience do you have in this field?

31. How would you describe your last boss?

32. How do you spend your spare time?

33. What do you know about this company?

34. Are you willing to begin at the entry level?

35. Are you authorized to work in this country?

36. How do you feel about teamwork?

37. What is your understanding of customer service?

38. Are you willing to work independently?

39. Are you prepared to learn new things?

40. What formal training have you had?

41. Are you willing to work evening and weekend hours?

42. How do you feel about a highly customer responsive assignment? Give an example.

43. What has been your experience with customer service?

44. Why do you want to come to work for us?

45. Tell me about your experiences with teamwork in your last job.

46. Tell me about a few of your key decision-making experiences in your last assignment.

47. What is best about you when you are working with others?

48. How do you feel about sharing your ideas with others?

49. How old are you?

50. We are a company focused on continuous improvement.
    What improvements have you made that effected a positive difference in your previous company or organization?

List at least 10 questions that you would ask an employment interviewer. Write down your anticipated response.

1. Question:
   Anticipated response from the interviewer:

2. Question:
   Anticipated response from the interviewer:

3. Question:
   Anticipated response from the interviewer:

4. Question:
   Anticipated response from the interviewer:

5. Question:
   Anticipated response from the interviewer:

6. Question:
   Anticipated response from the interviewer:

7. Question:
   Anticipated response from the interviewer:

8.   Question:
        Anticipated response from the interviewer:

9.   Question:
        Anticipated response from the interviewer:

10.   Question:
        Anticipated response from the interviewer:

Exercise 10

Practice Interview

Part 1:

Choose a partner. Decide who will be the interviewer and who will be the interviewee. Select questions from Exercise 9 to conduct a practice interview. Record your questions in the space provided below.

Remember, it is very important to maintain eye contact during the job interview. When playing the role of the interviewee, it is recommended that you look directly at the interviewer's nose. This approach is less confrontational than looking into a person's eyes.

Interviewer, write your questions and the interviewee's responses here.

Interviewer'sQuestions	Interviewee's Responses

Practice Interview

Part 2:

The employment applicant should prepare a list of questions to ask the interviewer. You should have your list of questions prepared. Ask your partner the questions you have prepared. Record all questions and responses in the space provided. Use a separate page if necessary.

Interviewer's Questions	Interviewee's Responses

TIP #10 AFTER YOUR EMPLOYMENT INTERVIE

After your visit, be sure to send a thank-you note to those who interviewed you. Keep the note brief, but be sure to reiterate your interest in the position, if that's the case. Even if you decide to take a different job, at a minimum, your note should thank that organization for its hospitality. Sending a thank-you letter may make you an unforgettable candidate. You may need to re-apply for a position with that company at a later time.

Sample Thank-you letter

Mary Jo Need a job
2223 Sisco Avenue
Freeport, VA 99000
(898) 999-0098

March 6, 2020

Mrs. Cecelia McDuffie
Human Resource Manager
4356 Statton Plaza
Freeport, VA 19887

Dear Mrs. McDuffie:

I want to thank you for interviewing me yesterday for the entry level Computer Operator position. I enjoyed meeting you and learning more about your company.

My enthusiasm for the position and my interest in working for your company were strengthened as a result of the interview. I think my education and training fit nicely with the job requirements, and I am sure that I could make a significant contribution to the organization over time.

I want to reiterate my strong interest in the position and in working with you and your staff. You provide the kind of opportunity I seek.

Please feel free to call me at (898) 999-0098 if I can provide you with additional information.

Again, thank you for the interview and your consideration.

Sincerely,
Mary Jo Need a job

Hint: A follow-up telephone call can be made if more than a week has passed since you have heard from the interviewer.

Sample Rejection Letter

You may be offered a job but you have decided to take another position with a different company. Write a thank-you (rejection letter) to the interviewer anyway. He/she may keep your résumé on file, and re-offer you a position at a later time.

Joe Outta Work
(000) 667-0098

8900 Pleasehelp Lane
Employment Line, NJ 99887

February 21, 1999

Ms. Cynthia Norvales
Hansel & Sons Delivery
1235 Narrowneck MA 87653

Dear Ms. Norvales:

Thank you very much for offering me the position of Commercial Truck Driver with your company.
You have a fine organization, and there are many aspects of the position which are very appealing to me. However, I believe it is in our mutual best interest that I decline your kind offer. This had been a difficult decision for me, but I believe it is the appropriate one for my career at this time.
I want to thank you for the consideration and courtesy given to me. It was a pleasure meeting you and your fine staff.

Sincerely,

Joe Outta Work

Exercise 11

Tip #10 – After the Interview

Use the space below to write a thank-you letter to a prospective employer. Remember to check your spelling, grammar, and punctuation. Refer to your Tips from your Job Coach textbook.

Exercise 12

<u>The Rejection Letter</u>

Use the space below to write a rejection letter to an interviewer. Remember to check your spelling, grammar, and punctuation. Refer to your Tips from your Job Coach textbook.

TIP #11 RECEIVING AN OFFER OF EMPLOYMENT

You may not be offered a job at the end of an interview. However, stay encouraged if the decision takes longer. The interviewer may want to check your references or interview others. You should be told when to expect an answer. If you have not been informed, you may ask if you can call back in a few days. In any case, remember to follow-up with a thank-you letter.

TIP #12 WHAT IF SOMEONE ELSE GETS HIRED?

You may have to go through many interviews before you get a job. This is true for most people throughout their careers. You should learn from each interview, even though someone else was hired. Think about what happened during the interview.

Did you have a specific job in mind when you applied?
Did you know something about the company's business?
Were you able to give good answers to all of the interviewer's questions?

If the answer to any of these questions is no, then perhaps you already know why someone else was hired. Sometimes, the reasons are complex. You could politely ask the interviewer why they made the decision to hire someone else. This information may be helpful on your next interview.

Another question you may ask yourself is "Do my skills need improvement?" If so, you need to polish up on your skills. What is most important is to stay encouraged. There is a job out there for you. You may need more time to find it. Send a thank-you note anyway. That interviewer may pass your résumé on!

TIP #13 WHAT EMPLOYERS EXPECT FROM EMPLOYEES

To come to work on time every day.
To work hard.
To follow company rules and policies.
To carry out orders.
To be willing to lend a helping hand whenever asked.
To appreciate privileges – not abuse them.
To be honest.
To be loyal.
To do the work correctly and complete it on time.
To take pride in their work and do it to the best of their ability.
To make an effort to improve.
To accept responsibility.

Exercise 13

Tip #13 – What Employers expect from Employees

List 12 things employers expect from employees. Explain each

1. ____.

2. ____.

3. ____.

4. ____.

5. ____.

6. ____.

7. ____.

8. ____ .

9. ____ .

10. ____ .

11. ____ .

12. ____ .

Exercise 14

What makes you valuable on the job?

Discuss the following items in detail.

What makes you valuable to your employer, the customer, to yourself, and to your future?

Know your responsibilities

Know your relationship to the customer

Do your job well

Be a team player and be willing to work independently

Be prepared to be flexible and creative in your assignment

Make your customer feel absolutely welcome

Make every day a success

Know customer expectations

Be on time

Be Dependable

I. **Know your responsibilities.**
Make sure that you have a thorough understanding of your responsibilities and carry them out to your fullest potential.

Know how your responsibilities contribute to the responsibilities of others.

II. **Know your relationship to the customer.**
How do you contribute to the delivery of services?
How often do you come face to face with customers?
How do you contribute to those who frequently come face to face with the customers?.

III.   **Do your job well.**
Be fantastic at what you do.
Through your performance, help others to know that you are the best at what you do.

Contribute to your success; and contribute to the success of your co-workers.

> To increase customer satisfaction.
> To increase productivity.
> To generate repeat customers.
> To generate new customers.

I.   **Be a team player and be willing to work independently.**
Be willing to share information with other team members.
Be willing to accept the ideas of others, in addition to your own.

II.   **Be prepared to be flexible and creative in your assignment.**
Be willing to accept change.
Be willing to make change work in a positive direction.

III.   **Make your customer feels absolutely welcome.**
Be a good listener.
Be accommodating.

IV.   **Make every day a success.**
Be good enough for accurate performance.
Be flexible enough for successful performance.

V.   **Know customer expectations.**
Learn what you need to do to satisfy your responsibilities.
Connect your responsibilities to customer expectations.

VI.   **Be on time.**
Be on time with your performance so that your performance can contribute to cost expectations.
Timeliness is important to the delivery of service.
Arrive to work on time.
Arrive back from your break on time.

IV.   **Be Dependable.**
When you promise to deliver, deliver what you promise.
Let others know through your performance that you can be depended on.

TIP #14 YOUR CREDIT REPORT

For Employment Purposes

Employers may view and use a modified version of your credit report. It is used to help assess an applicant's character. Some employers use credit reports when considering promotions. You must give a prospective employer your permission; and you will be asked to sign a separate document acknowledging that they will be obtaining your credit report. Current employers may review your report only if you have given permission as part of your employment. The report that employers receive does not contain account numbers, your year of birth and your spouse's name. Employers are not permitted to ask those questions; and the report does not show that information. This is done to comply with federal employment laws. Should you know there might be credit issues, it is best to be forthcoming and explain these issues to your perspective employer.

Activity 1

Choose twenty words from Appendix 3 to write 20 descriptive sentences about yourself. Share your sentences with your classmates.

From the twenty descriptive sentences you just wrote, rewrite the sentences that begins with "I." Write about yourself objectively, as though you were thinking of a different individual. Write descriptively about yourself without using the word "I." Think in terms of skill rather than self. Use these descriptive sentences when writing your résumé.

Activity 2

Changes

____

____

____

____

____

____

____

____

____

____

____

____

____

____

Change your behavior

Change your focus, change your behavior, change your future.
Every morning I get out of bed.

I eat breakfast.
I leave for work.
I walk down my street.
I turn the corner.
I fall into a hole.
I get hurt.

What can I do differently so that I will not get hurt every morning?
Write your response here before turning the page.

____
____
____
____
____
____.

Activity 2   *Solution suggestions*

Changes
<u>Change your behavior</u>

Change your focus, change your behavior, change your future.
Every morning I get out of bed.
I eat breakfast.
I leave for work.
I walk down my street.
I turn the corner.
I fall into a hole.
I get hurt.

What can I do differently so that I will not get hurt every morning?

Walk up the street.
Keep walking straight.
Turn down a different street.
Walk around the hole.
Catch the bus.
Drive your car to work.
Arrange for someone to pick you up for wor
Take a taxi cab.

Activity 3

Changes
<u>Change your behavior</u>

Change your focus, change your behavior, change your future.

I leave for work at the same time each morning.
I catch the same bus each morning.
The same man is on the bus.
He says hello in the same way each morning.
He then says something nasty to me each morning.
I hang my head in shame each morning.

I arrive at work feeling depressed and upset.
I go through the day thinking of what he said to me.
I feel bad all day long.

What can I do differently so that I will not feel bad each morning?

Write your response here before turning the page.

____
____
____
____
________________________________.

Activity 3   *Solution suggestions*

Changes
<u>Change your behavior</u>

Change your focus, change your behavior, change your future.
I leave for work at the same time each morning.

I catch the same bus each morning.
The same man is on the bus.
He says hello in the same way each morning.
He then says something nasty to me each morning.
I hang my head in shame each morning.
I arrive at work feeling depressed and upset.
I go through the day thinking of what he said to me.
I feel bad all day long.

What can I do differently so that I will not feel bad each morning?

Catch an earlier bus.
Take the train instead of the bus.
Say hello, and find something to read.
Ignore the man.
Tell him that you don't appreciate the nasty comments.
Express concern about his low self-esteem.
Tell him about your positive qualities.
Think pleasant thoughts after he says hello.
Focus on your goals instead of letting his comments get the best of you.
Say something pleasant to the man to redirect his thinking in a positive direction.

Activity 4

Changes
<u>Flexibility</u>

Change your focus, change your behavior, change your future.

I only had a piece of toast for breakfast; that's all there was time for.
I'm at my job site.
My supervisor has announced a mandatory meeting immediately after lunch.
It's time for my lunch break, and I can barely wait to eat a fat juicy burger and a side of fries!
My co-worker is late coming back to relieve me.
It's now 15 minutes into my lunch break.
I must be back at my work site on time.
My co-worker has yet to arrive.
My lunch break is over.
I must attend the meeting.
I am hungry.
I am frustrated.
I am angry.
What shall I do to let my co-worker know that I too needed to eat my lunch?

Write your response here before turning the page.

____
____
____
____
____.

Activity 4   *Solution suggestions*

Changes
<u>Flexibility</u>

Change your focus, change your behavior, change your future.

I only had a piece of toast for breakfast; that's all there was time for.
I'm at my job site.
My supervisor has announced a mandatory meeting immediately after lunch.
It's time for my lunch break, and I can barely wait to eat a fat juicy burger and a side of fries!
My co-worker is late coming back to relieve me.
It's now 15 minutes into my lunch break.
I must be back at my site on time.
My co-worker has yet to arrive.
My lunch break is over.
I must attend the meeting.
I am hungry.
I am frustrated.
I am angry.

What shall I do to let my co-worker know that I too needed to eat my lunch?

Five minutes before your lunch break, tell your supervisor that your co-worker has yet to return from break.
Ask your supervisor if there is someone else to relieve you.
Tell your co-worker to return from break on time in the future.
Ask your supervisor if the meeting can be postponed until after you've eaten your lunch.
Ask your supervisor if you can take your lunch break after the meeting.
Go to a private area, at your first chance, and take a few moments to calm down.

Activity 5

Changes
Know customer expectations
Know your responsibilities
Be dependable
Be a team player

Change your focus, change your behavior, change your future.
I work in a fast food restaurant.
A woman came in.
I greeted her with a smile and asked, "May I help you?"
She ordered a sandwich, hold the mayo, hold the pickles.
I put the order through.
The woman paid me; I gave her the sandwich and her change.
She thanked me.
I told her to have a nice day.
The woman came back to the counter and yelled, "I told you to hold the mayo and the pickles, there are both mayo and pickles on my sandwich! Can't you do this job right?"
I felt bad.
I knew I told the cook to hold the mayo and pickles.
What can I do to assure customer satisfaction in the future?

Write your response here before turning the page.

____
____
____
____
_______________________________________.

Activity 5   *Solution suggestions*

Changes

Know customer expectations
Know your responsibilities
Be dependable
Be a team player

Change your focus, change your behavior, change your future.

I work in a fast food restaurant.
A woman came in.
I greeted her with a smile and asked, "May I help you?"
She ordered a sandwich, hold the mayo, hold the pickles.
I put the order through.
The woman paid me; I gave her the sandwich and her change.
She thanked me.
I told her to have a nice day.

The woman came back to the counter and yelled, "I told you to hold the mayo and the pickles, there are both mayo and pickles on my sandwich! Can't you do this job right?"
I felt bad.
I knew I told the cook to hold the mayo and pickles.
What can I do to assure customer satisfaction in the future?
Apologize to the customer. Tell her that she will have the correct item immediately.
Reorder the sandwich from the cook.
Thank the customer again, and assure her that it will not happen again.
Speak to the cook. Let him/her know that his job performance has an impact on your customer service and customer satisfaction.
Ask the cook to examine the food orders carefully in the future.
Ask your supervisor to speak to the cook if this performance continues.

Activity 6

Changes

Be dependable
Be on time
Be prepared to be flexible and creative in your assignment
Be flexible

Change your focus, change your behavior, change your future.
My boss, Mr. Booney, has an important meeting with a client.
Mr. Booney asked me to prepare a report for the client.
It's nearly time for me to go home.
I'm almost finished printing out the report.
The printer is out of ink.
That was the last ink cartridge!

This is an important client!
I panic!
I must get this report to Mr. Booney immediately!

What can I do to get the report to Mr. Booney in time for the meeting?

Write your response here before turning the page.

____
____
____
____
____.

Activity 6   *Solution suggestions*

Changes

Be dependable
Be on time

Be prepared to be flexible and creative in your assignment
Be flexible

Change your focus, change your behavior, change your future.
My boss, Mr. Booney, has an important meeting with a client
Mr. Booney asked me to prepare a report for the client.
It's nearly time for me to go home.
I'm almost finished printing out the report.
The printer is out of ink.
That was the last ink cartridge!
This is an important client!
I panic!
I must get this report to Mr. Booney immediately!

What can I do to get the report to Mr. Booney in time for the meeting?

Ask someone in a different department if they have an ink cartridge that you could use.
Call a store and ask them to deliver an ink cartridge to your office.
Tell Mr. Booney that the report may be late and explain the reason.
Prepare to stay as long as it takes to complete the report.
Calm down.

Activity 7

Situation 1

<u>An employment interview</u>

Mrs. Charles supervises the auditors division of a major corporation. She needed to hire an assistant to help with the front office. She called a temporary employment firm because she wanted to hire on a temporary basis at first, and then offer the vacancy as a full-time position with benefits.

Mrs. Charles required a reliable incumbent. The individual needed to possess effective oral and written communication skills, and entry-level computer skills. The applicant needed to have interpersonal skills in order to communicate with clients via telephone and in person. She needed a self-motivated individual who required little supervision – someone who is able to learn the accounting software packages quickly and apply it effectively.

The temporary agency assured Mrs. Charles that Nina was perfect for the job. She was reliable, dependable, trainable, willing to learn, eager to work, punctual, and possessed effective communication skills.

Mrs. Charles invited Nina in for a personal interview at 9:30 a.m. on Tuesday. Nina, wearing a navy blue business suit, arrived at 9:15 a.m., and waited in the outside office. While waiting, she reviewed her résumé and her pre-planned questions. Nina noticed the company's Mission Statement hanging on the wall. She read it, studied it, and prepared more questions to ask Mrs. Charles during the interview.

At 9:30, Mrs. Charles opened her office door and introduced herself to Nina. Nina stood up and extended her hand while she introduced herself. She looked directly at Mrs. Charles' nose as she spoke. Mrs. Charles invited Nina into the office and offered her a seat. Nina waited until Mrs. Charles sat down before she sat in the chair positioned on the opposite side of the desk

Mrs. Charles offered small talk while she observed Nina's posture and mannerism. Nina observed the certificates on the wall behind the desk, the photographs on the desk and shelves, and the wooden sculpture positioned in the corner of the large office.

Mrs. Charles informed Nina of the responsibilities the vacant position required. She explained the importance of reliability, dependability, and communication skills. Mrs. Charles explained that because she was responsible for financial transactions and audits, the documents were highly sensitive and required security clearance. Mrs. Charles further explained the importance of confidentiality, telling Nina that she should not discuss the details of the position with anyone. Nina communicated a clear understanding of what Mrs. Charles required; and the interview continued.

Mrs. Charles asked Nina for her résumé. Nina handed her one, while keeping one for herself. As she reviewed the résumé, Mrs. Charles made notes in the side margin. She wanted Nina to expound on her experiences. Nina was asked why she had left the meat manufacturing plant where she was an office clerk. Nina responded confidently, and explained that she needed more challenge and responsibility. She told Mrs. Charles that she wanted to utilize her accounting skills. When asked if she was familiar with a specific computer accounting software, Nina told Mrs. Charles that although she had no experience with that particular software, she was very familiar with a similar software.

Mrs. Charles wanted to know if Nina was able to work flexible hours because, at times, working past 5:00 p.m. would be required. Nina assured Mrs. Charles that working past 5:00 p.m. on occasion wouldn't be a problem as long as she was given advance notice. When asked what her career goals were, Nina explained that she wanted to complete her associates degree in business within the next three years, and advance her status in her work place.

Mrs. Charles asked Nina to demonstrate how she would handle multiple tasks, such as a client in the waiting room while the phone continuously rang, and she had to post payroll out by noon. Nina said that she would handle the client first, put the phone calls on hold in the order by which they were received. After she directed the client, she would route the telephone calls, and then work on posting the payroll. Mrs. Charles invited Nina to ask questions about the company and about her responsibilities.

Nina asked Mrs. Charles what employees seem to like best about the company. Mrs. Charles responded by saying that the company offers a terrific benefit package, which included, among other things, an annual eye exam, biannual dental exams, and full medical coverage.

The company also offers overtime hours at time and a half pay.

Next, Nina asked what the long-range possibilities for employees in similar positions who consistently perform above expectation were. Mrs. Charles explained the company's policy of promotion from within, as well as the extensive training programs available for all employees.

Nina told Mrs. Charles that she had read the company's Mission Statement hanging on the wall of the outer office. She asked what the statement "Our environmental performance represents the collective work of many dedicated employees" meant.

Mrs. Charles replied that the company's success depends on the ability to effectively manage both the need for environmental protection and the need for economic development. She expounded by saying that this can only happen if the technicians and the management team work cohesively to ensure a high quality of service to the customers. She also stated that clients depend on the company for support; that the company deliver services to both businesses and residents. She concluded by saying that it is imperative to deliver services in a timely and professional manner.

Mrs. Charles seemed pleased with Nina's responses, as well as her questions. She offered her the temporary position for ten weeks at $13.00 per hour. Nina thanked Mrs. Charles for her offer, and asked for a few days to consider the position. Mrs. Charles told her that she needed someone immediately but gave her until tomorrow afternoon for her decision.

Nina went home and considered the offer. She decided that a ten-week temporary position that could lead to full time employment doing something she enjoyed was exactly what she needed. She felt she would be challenged by the responsibilities, and that the work offered room for training and advancement. In any case, Nina would have the opportunity to learn new technology, acquire new skills and a new experience to add to her résumé.

Nina called Mrs. Charles the next morning and informed her of her decision to accept the position.

Answer the following questions:

1. Was the interview successful for Mrs. Charles? Why/why not?

____
____
____.

2. Was the interview successful for Nina? Why/why not?

____
____
____.

3. What were the responsibilities of the incumbent of the vacant position?

____
____
____.

4. Why did Nina review her résumé while waiting in the outer office?

____
____
____.

5   In what way did Nina prepare for the employment interview?

____

____

____.

6   Why did Nina observe personal items in Mrs. Charles' office?

____

____

____.

7   Why did Mrs. Charles observe Nina's mannerism and posture?

____

____

____.

8   Why did Mrs. Charles write notes on Nina's résumé?

____

____

____.

9   Why did Nina keep a copy of her résumé for herself during the interview?

____

____

____.

10.   Nina asked Mrs. Charles about the long-range possibilities for employees with the company. What was the purpose of Nina's question?

____

____

____.

11.   In addition to extracting information from Nina, why did Mrs. Charles ask Nina to explain why she left the meat manufacturing plant?

____

____

____.

12.   Why is reliability and dependability an important part of this vacant position?

____

____

____.

12.   Why is reliability and dependability an important part of this vacant position?

____
____
____.

13.   Why is communication skills an important part of this vacant position?

____
____
____.

14.   When Mrs. Charles informed Nina of the necessity to work overtime, what was she trying to find out?

____
____
____.

Activity 8

Situation 2

<u>Diversity</u>

Ms. Green's refrigerator was leaking water. She had purchased the refrigerator two years ago. She did not understand why it was leaking now. She called the company from which she purchased the appliance.

"Hello, my refrigerator is not working properly. Can you please send a technician out to repair it?" Ms. Green inquired.
"Just a moment. I need to get some information from you.
What is your name and address?" the customer service representative responded.

"Cynthia Green, 3345 Seymore Avenue. My refrigerator is leaking water, and the light went out. I've unplugged it to avoid an electrical shock."

"Good, Ms. Green. It's a good idea to unplug a utility that is leaking. I see your warranty is still in effect. I'll put in a work order for a technician to take a look at it. When would be best for you, morning or afternoon?" the customer service representative asked.

"Immediately! My food is spoiling as we speak," Ms. Green exclaimed.

"OK, Ms. Green, calm down. I'll post your request for a technician immediately. Someone should be there within the hour to make the repair," said the customer service representative.

"Thank you. I'll be waiting," Ms. Green said calmly.

John, a technician, received the order. He had just completed a repair order on an electrical line.

This was a difficult situation, but he made the repairs. Now, he is responding to Ms. Green's call.

"Hello, Mrs. Cynthia Green?" asked John.

"Yes. Are you here to repair my refrigerator?" asked Ms. Green.

"Yes, Mrs. Green, what seems to be the problem?" John waited at the door until he was invited in.

"Please, come into the kitchen. Right this way," Ms. Green said, leading John to the kitchen.

John couldn't help but notice the filth in the house. There were dirty dishes, piles of clothes, and roaches. He was hesitant about going any further, but he did. When he reached the kitchen, he saw roaches scatter on the floor, counter top, and table.

John decided not to do the job. He promptly left Ms. Green's house.

"I'm sorry, Ms. Green, but I cannot do this job," John said as he left the house.

Answer the following questions:

1. Did John's decision have anything to do with his previous work order? Explain.

____
____
____
____
____.

2. How did John's decision not to service Ms. Green impact his company?

____
____
____
____
____.

3. How do you think Ms. Green felt?

____
____
____
____
____.

4. Did John make assumptions about Ms. Green? Explain.

____
____
____
____
____.

Ms. Green was very upset that the technician left without even looking at her refrigerator. She called the company back, and informed them that he had left without making any repairs.

"Ms. Green, I apologize for that technician's behavior. He should have made the repairs while he was there," the customer service representative explained.

"My refrigerator is still not working. My food is spoiling, and my kitchen floor is flooded.

What are you going to do about it?" Ms. Green asked.

"I will call his supervisor, and report the problem. There will be a technician at your home within the hour, Ms. Green. The problem will be dealt with immediately," said the customer service representative.

"Thank you, and hurry!" Ms. Green exclaimed.

John had called his supervisor ahead. He told her of the roach infested house, and explained why he refused to make the repair to the refrigerator.

"John, you meet me at Ms. Green's house in one half hour. You are going to service this customer with professionalism," said Mrs. Hill.

"But the place was swarming with roaches everywhere!" John exclaimed.

"You were hired to do a job. Ms. Green's contract is still in effect. We will honor it," Mrs. Hill told John.

"I don't want to work in that part of town again. I don't want to service that type of customer," John declared.

"Be at Ms. Green's house in one half hour," Mrs. Hill said adamantly.

John met his supervisor at Ms. Green's house. Mrs. Hill rang the doorbell.

"Hello, Ms. Green?" Mrs. Hill asked.

"Yes, I'm Ms. Green. What is he doing here? He said he wouldn't work on my refrigerator," Ms. Green said.

"I apologize for John's attitude. He is one of our better technicians," Mrs. Hill explained.

"I'm sorry, Ms. Green. It's been a long day. I was tired and irritable. I should have made the repair when I was here earlier," John explained.

"Okay, you know where the kitchen is. Please fix my refrigerator," Ms. Green hesitantly said.

John pushed the refrigerator away from the wall. He saw more roaches, both dead and alive.

"Please excuse the roaches," said Ms. Green. "The exterminator will be here later on today. I've been having a problem with roaches for the past week. I think my neighbor had her house exterminated; and now they're all over my house. I just finished my lunch, and I was about to do my laundry when I heard this loud noise and smelled something funny coming from the kitchen. Then, all of this water started to come from the refrigerator. I opened the refrigerator door, and the light bulb blew out. I unplugged the refrigerator and called you."

"Well, it's a good thing you called when you did. We'll see what the problem is. Then, John will fix it," Mrs. Hill said.

John examined the back of the refrigerator, made an assessment of the problem, and made the repair.

"Would you care for a glass of water?" Ms. Green asked.

"No, thanks," replied John.

"Yes, I would," replied Mrs. Hill. "The weather is brutally hot today."

Mrs. Hill sat at the kitchen table, and drank the glass of water.

Answer the following questions:

1.   Why do you think Mrs. Hill was adamant about servicing Ms. Green's refrigerator?

____
____
____
____.

2.   How did Ms. Green feel when she saw Mrs. Hill and John at her door?

____
____
____
____.

3.   How was the customer service representative helpful?

____

____

____

____.

4.   What would have been the outcome if Mrs. Hill had agreed with John?

____

____

____

____.

5.   It is obvious that John needs some improvement. In what area(s) should he receive additional training?

____

____

____

____.

6.   If you were John, how would you have handled the situation?

____

____

____

____.

7.   If you were Mrs. Hill, how would you have handled the situation?

____

____

____

____.

Appendix 1

The Employment Application

Use a black ball point pen to complete the following employment applications. Employers need to file the employment application. Neatness counts.

APPLICATION FOR EMPLOYMENT

PRE-EMPLOYMENT QUESTIONNAIRE
EQUAL OPPORTUNITY EMPLOYER

PERSONAL INFORMATION   DATE : ________________________

NAME (LAST NAME FIRST)			SOCIAL SECURITY NO.
PRESENT ADDRESS	CITY	STATE	ZIP CODE
PERMANENT ADDRESS	CITY	STATE	ZIP CODE
PHONE NO. ( )		REFERRED BY	

EMPLOYMENT DESIRED

POSITION	DATE YOU CAN START	SALARY DESIRED
ARE YOU EMPLOYED? YES ☐ NO ☐	IF SO, MAY WE INQUIRE OF YOUR PRESENT EMPLOYER? ☐ YES ☐ NO	
EVER APPLIED TO THIS COMPANY BEFORE? YES NO	WHERE?	WHEN?

EDUCATION

NAME AND LOCATION OF SCHOOL	YEARS ATTENDED	DID YOU GRADUATE?	SUBJECTS STUDIED
GRAMMAR SCHOOL			
HIGH SCHOOL			
COLLEGE			
TRADE, BUSINESS OR CORRESPON-DENCE SCHOOL			

GENERAL

SUBJECTS OF SPECIAL STUDY/RESEARCH WORK OR SPECIAL TRAINING/SKILLS		
U.S. MILITARY OR NAVAL SERVICE	RANK	

FORMER EMPLOYERS

DATE MONTH AND YEAR				
FROM				
TO				
FROM				
TO				
FROM				
TO				
FROM				
TO				

REFERENCES

GIVE THE NAMES OF THREE PERSONS NOT RELATED TO YOU WHOM YOU HAVE KNOWN AT LEAST ONE YEAR.

	NAME	ADDRESS	BUSINESS	YEARS KNOWN
1.				
2.				
3.				

AUTHORIZATION

"I CERTIFY THAT THE FACTS CONTAINED IN THIS APPLICATON ARE TRUE AND COMPLETE TO THE BEST OF MY KNOWLEDGE. I UNDERSTAND THAT, IF EMPLOYED, FALSIFIED STATEMENTS ON THIS APPLICATION SHALL BE GROUNDS FOR DISMISSAL.

I AUTHORIZE INVESTIGATION OF ALL STATEMENTS CONTAINED HEREIN; AND THE REFERENCES AND EMPLOYERS LISTSED ABOVE; ANY AND ALL INFORMATION CONCERNING MY PREVIOUS EMPLOYMENT, AND ANY PERTINENT INFORMATION THEY MAY HAVE, PERSONAL OR OTHERWISE. I RELEASE THE COMPANY FROM ALL LIABILITY FOR ANY DAMAGE THAT MAY RESULT FROM UTILIZATION OF SUCH INFORMATION.

I ALSO UNDERSTAND AND AGREE THAT NO REPRESENTATIVE OF THE COMPANY HAS ANY AUTHORITY TO ENTER INTO ANY AGREEMENT FOR EMPOLYMENT FOR ANY SPECIFIED PERIOD OF TIME, OR TO MAKE ANY AGREEMENT CONTRARY TO THE FOREGOING, UNLESS IT IS IN WRITING AND SIGNED BY AN AUTHORIZED COMPANY REPRESENTATIVE."

DATE_______________________________________SIGNATURE____.

INTERVIEWED BY____DATE-______________________________

--DO NOT WRITE BELOW THIS LINE --

NEATNESS			CHARACTER	
PERSONALITY			ABILITY	
HIRED	FOR DEPT.	POSITION	WILL REPORT	SALARY WAGES

APPROVED:

1.________________________________2.________________________________3.________________________________

EMPLOYMENT MANAGER   DEPT. HEAD   GENERAL MANAGER

Appendix 2

Employers must prove to the government that their employees have the right to work in the United States. It is necessary for employers to report all new employees to the immigration and Naturalization Service. Your new employer will ask that you provide proof of eligibility to work in the United States. To prove you are legally eligible to work in the United States, you must provide two types of identification. A birth certificate, a social security number, a green card, a driver's license are all legitimate and acceptable proof of identification. You will be required to complete the form below before you begin your new job.

Complete the sample Immigration and Naturalization Service Employment Eligibility Verification form below.

Immigration and Naturalization Service Employment Eligibility Verification
Please read instructions carefully before completing this form. The instructions must be available during completion of this form. ANTI-DISCRIMINATION NOTICE. It is illegal to discriminate against work eligible individuals. Employers CANNOT specify which document(s) they will accept from an employee. The refusal to hire an individual because of a future expiration date may also constitute illegal discrimination.

Section 1. Employee Information and Verification.			To be completed and signed by employee at the time employment begins.	
Print Name: Last	First	**Middle Initial**	**Maiden Name**	
Address (Street Name and Number)		**Apt. #**	**Date of birth (month/day/year**	
City	**State**	**Zip Code**	**Social Security #**	

I am aware that federal law provides for imprisonment and/or fines for false statements or use of false documents in connection with the completion of this form.	I attest under penalty of perjury that I am (check one of the following: A citizen or national of the United States A lawful Permanent resident (Alien of A _______ An alien authorized to work until _______ / / _______ Alien # or Admission # ____ _______ _______
Employer's Signature	Date (month/day/year)

Preparer and/or Translator Certification. (To be completed and signed if Section 1 is prepared by a person other than the employee) I attest, under penalty of perjury, that I have assisted in the completion of this form and that to the best of my knowledge the information is true and correct.

Preparer's Signature	**Print Name**
Address (Street Name and Number, City, State, Zip code)	**Date (month/day/year)**

Section 2. Employee Review and Verification. To be completed and signed by employer. Examine one docment from List B and one form List C as listed on the reverse of this form and record the type, number and expiration date, if any on the document(s).

List A   List B   AND   List C

Document Title _______________   OR

Issuing authority _______________

Document # _______________

Expiration Date (If Any) __/__/__

Document # _______________

Expiration Date (If Any) __/__/__

CERTIFICATION - I attest, under penalty of perjury, that I have examined the document(s) presented by the above named employee, that the above listed document(s) appear to be genuine and to relate to the employee named, that the employee began employment on (month/day/year) __/__/__ and that to the best of my knowledge the employee is eligible to work in the United states. (State employment agencies may omit the date the employee began employment).

Signature of Employer or Authorized Representative	Print Name	Title
Business Organization Name Address (Street Name and Number, City, State, Zip code)		Date

Employment Search Follow-Up Form

This is the beginning of your job search. All that's left is for you to do is to get organized, and get started. Good luck!

Organize your search for employment. Make several copies of this form to keep track of your search for employment.

Name of Company

____
Location

____
Telephone number   **Fax**   **E-mail**

____
Type of business

Vacant position(s)

____
____
____

How did you learn about the vacancy? ___________word of mouth
___________classified ad   ___________internet ad
___________networking   ___________job fair
___________yellow pages   ___________in person

When did you learn about the vacancy (date)
Have you contacted the company? ___________________   when? ___________________
Have you set the interview?
Date of interview? ______________ **Time of interview**______________
Name of interviewer____
Interviewer's title ____
What do you know about the company?

____
____

Questions to ask during the interview.

____
____
____
____

Date and time of the second interview.

____
____

Second interviewer's name and title.

____

____

How to contact second interviewer.

____

____

Were you hired? ______________   yes _____________
What could you do differently the next time?

Embrace Change

If you learn to view change as a natural occurrence, you can anticipate it and plan for it. Welcome change in your life. Just as bread can never become wheat and no fruit can become a flower. The future is ours to experience. We must continually ask "What will happen if…?" Change is life, and life is forever changing.
– Dona Woodley

About the Author

Dona Woodley is a middle child raised in Philadelphia, PA. She is a product of the Philadelphia public school system. Dona graduated with a Bachelorette of Education from the University of Pittsburgh in 1976. She earned her Masters of Special Education in 1981 from Antioch University. She taught special education in public school districts for 37 years before taking an early retirement.

During the course of her career, Dona took a position at a vocational high school in Pennsylvania. She was hired as a Job Coach. The position had no job description so Ms. Woodley invented one.